To ___________________

From ___________________

you are
so
loved

all you
NEED IS
Love

with you
FOREVER

you are
so
loved

all you
NEED IS
Love

Love
is all
Around

hugs
AND
KISSES

with you
FOREVER

all you
NEED IS
Love

Love
is all
Around

with you
FOREVER

I ♥ U

you are
so
loved

all you
NEED IS
Love

with you
FOREVER

you are
so
loved

all you
NEED IS
Love

with you
FOREVER

you are
so
loved

all you
NEED IS
Love

hugs
AND
KISSES

you are
so
loved

all you
NEED IS
Love

Love
is all
Around

Love

hugs
AND
KISSES

with you
FOREVER

you are
so
loved

all you
NEED IS
Love

hugs
AND
KISSES

with you
FOREVER

you are
so
loved

all you
NEED IS
Love

Love
is all
Around

you are
so
loved

all you
NEED IS
Love

you are
so
loved

all you
NEED IS
Love

hugs
AND
KISSES

with you
FOREVER

Love

you are
so
loved

all you
NEED IS
Love

Love
is all
Around

Time to head back to
Amazon to order
another book. If you
enjoyed this notebook,
we hope you will
share your opinion
by leaving a review
on Amazon.
Thank you,
Love Notes Press